RONALD DAUGHERTY

# STRUGGLED
## BUT
# *Favored*

A Journey of Faith Through Life's Toughest Battles

RONALD DAUGHERTY

# STRUGGLED
BUT
## Favored

A Journey of Faith Through Life's Toughest Battles

MEWE
Lithonia, GA

Scripture references are taken from the King James Version of
the Holy Bible unless otherwise noted.
Pronouns for referring to the Father, Son and Holy Spirit are
capitalized intentionally and the words satan and devil are
never capitalized.

Publisher:
More Excellent Way Enterprises
www.mewellc.com

Struggled but Favored
First Edition
ISBN: 979-8-9928362-0-2

Library of Congress Control Number: 2025906486

Printed in the United States of America

*I dedicate this book, my life story, to my mom—whose love never changed from the pain of disappointment to the joy of success.*

# TABLE OF CONTENTS

# FOREWORD

Ronald Daugherty, in his faith-filled book *Struggled but Favored*, takes readers on a journey through every emotion a human being can experience. You will find yourself in tears as you witness moments of deep despair, yet your faith will soar as you see how God came through just when it seemed like the end. Ronald's story is a powerful testament to divine intervention, leaving you with a sense of hope that is unspeakable and full of grace. THIS IS A MUST-READ—one that will undoubtedly inspire you to step into your purpose NOW!

Dr. Ruth W. Smith
Light of the World Covenant Fellowship International
*Founder and President*

Light of the World Christian University
*Founder and President*

Light of the World Christian Tabernacle International
*Co-Founder and President*

# INTRODUCTION

One day, I was chatting with a lifelong friend, reminiscing about the twists and turns of my journey. We had known each other since Head Start—what's now considered kindergarten. As we reflected on my life, he looked at me and said, "Bro, you got it." He wasn't just making conversation; he meant that I had a story worth telling. A story of struggle, resilience, and undeniable favor. I shared with him how I went from being the child who fell out of a moving car to the gospel preacher whom God carried across the world. He listened, nodding in agreement, as if he already knew that my testimony was more than just a personal reflection—it was a message meant for others.

*Struggled but Favored* is a journey through life's highest peaks and lowest valleys. It will take you from the innocence of childhood to the reckless confidence of youth, from dreaming big to making choices that led to a prison cell. But that prison cell became my turning point, launching a faith and freedom journey that changed everything. This book will move you to tears, stir your emotions, and leave you questioning the power of purpose and redemption. It's a story of how a person can face unimaginable trauma yet rise above it, a testament to the love of family, and a reflection on the deep impact of culture. Through it all, one truth remains—no matter the struggle, God's favor is still at work.

Ronald Daugherty

# Chapter 1

# The Beginning

## My Birth and the Start of Life's Struggles

My name's Ronald Daugherty, born October 7, 1959, at Grady Memorial Hospital in Atlanta, GA. The stories about my early years always fascinated me, even if they were told in bits and pieces by my family. One story that stood out was about a big accident I had as a little boy. I was told that I fell out of a moving car and fractured my skull. It was a miracle I survived, but I didn't come out of it unscathed. The aftermath left me with splitting headaches that were so intense, I couldn't even lift my head off the pillow some days. My family didn't have much, but they did what they could to help me cope.

I remember being carried around the house because walking was sometimes too much to bear. My aunt, Agnes Kelly, was always there, making me feel special in a world where I often felt fragile. She would kiss me on the forehead, her way of showing love and maybe even trying to heal me in her own way. Aunt Agnes had a way of making everything seem like it was going to be alright. Her husband,

Uncle Bill, would take me out to the porch, gently rocking me back and forth in an old wooden chair. That creaking sound of the rocker is something I can still hear in my memories, a simple comfort in a complicated world.

One of the most vivid memories from that time was a family trip to a dairy farm. All the kids around me were full of energy, running around, giggling, trying to milk the cows. I wanted to join them so badly, but there I was, lying in Harriet Guthrie's lap, the pounding in my head making it impossible to even sit up straight. The sounds of laughter filled the air, but they felt distant, almost like I was listening to them from underwater. That was one of those moments when I realized my childhood was different from other kids'. But I wasn't bitter, just curious why things were the way they were.

## My Family and Growing Pains

The headaches seemed to last forever, but eventually, I grew out of them, or maybe I just learned to live with the pain. Either way, by the time I was old enough for first grade, life started throwing new challenges my way. My oldest sister developed serious heart issues. The doctors said she had leaky valves and needed surgery right away. My parents were stressed, scrambling to get her the care she needed. They took her up to Minnesota for the operation, which meant I had to stay behind. I ended up living with my first-grade teacher, Ms. Jackson, in Lithonia, GA. She was a tough lady, real no-nonsense, but she looked after me like I was her own. Every morning, she made sure I was up, dressed, and ready for school, with a packed lunch in my hand.

It was a strange time, living with someone who wasn't family, but Ms. Jackson did her best to make me feel at home. I would sit at her kitchen table, eating grits and scrambled eggs, listening to her talk about the importance of education. "Ronald, if you want to make something of yourself, you gotta learn how to read and write properly," she would say, her eyes peering over her glasses. I didn't fully understand it then, but she was planting seeds that would grow in me much later.

When my parents finally came home, I was beyond happy. I remember that Easter Sunday like it was yesterday. My little sister and I were dressed to the nines, sitting in my grandmother's living room, waiting to head out to church. My sister was still recovering, but seeing her smile was like seeing a ray of sunshine after a long, dark storm. For a moment, life felt almost normal again.

## Finding Strength in Sports

As I got older, my headaches started fading, replaced by a love for sports that seemed to come out of nowhere. I was a natural athlete, or at least that's what everyone told me. Football, basketball, baseball—you name it, I played it. The adrenaline rush of running down the field, the sound of a basketball swishing through the net, the crack of a bat hitting a ball—I loved it all. I was fast, often the quickest one on the field, which earned me a spot playing with kids who were older than me. My uncle

Rick, who was only three years older, was always there to push me, sometimes harder than I wanted, but it made me better.

Playing sports gave me something I desperately needed—an escape. I wasn't just the kid with the headaches anymore; I was Ronald, the athlete. When I hit the field, I felt powerful, like I could conquer anything. That confidence spilled over into other areas of my life. Eventually, I started playing with kids my own age, and for the first time, I felt like I truly belonged. It wasn't just about winning games; it was about finding my place in the world.

Around the age of 12, I started working for my dad and my Uncle Willie James in their masonry business. It was hard work, especially for someone my age, but it was a rite of passage in our family. I would spend long hours under the hot Georgia sun, mixing cement, stacking bricks, and learning the trade. Those were some of the toughest but most formative years of my life. My dad was strict, expecting nothing less than perfection, but I knew it was his way of preparing me for the real world.

## My First Taste of Trouble

It was also around this time that I had my first taste of alcohol. My cousin Stan had just come back from Vietnam, full of stories and wild energy. One day, he handed me a bottle of Strawberry Hill wine, with that devilish grin on his face, and told me to take a swig. I was hesitant, but I did it. Before I knew it, I was drunk, stumbling around, thinking I was invincible. My dad and uncle were furious when they found out, but deep down, I think they knew it was just part of growing up. That didn't stop them from giving me a good talking-to, though.

Despite the reprimands, there was something about that experience that made me feel like I was stepping into a new chapter of my life. I was no longer just a kid; I was starting to see the world through a different lens. Drinking became a way to prove I was tough, to show the older boys that I could hang. But looking back, I realize it was more than that. It was my way of coping with everything—my health issues, my family's struggles, the pressures of growing up too fast.

The challenges and setbacks of my early years were just the beginning of a long journey. Each moment, from the farm trips to the football fields, shaped who I was becoming. I was learning that life didn't come with an easy path, but I was determined to make my own way, no matter the odds.

# Chapter 2

# A Taste of the Streets

## Early Encounters with Temptation

By the time I turned 13, life had already thrown me some serious curveballs. My mom and dad had split up, and it was like the ground beneath my feet had shifted. With my dad out of the picture, I found myself with a lot more freedom, maybe too much of it.

My mom was busy trying to keep things together, so I had more leeway to get into whatever I wanted. I quickly learned that I could get away with just about anything around her. There weren't many rules left to follow, and even if there were, nobody was enforcing them.

One of those nights, I stayed over with a friend of my older sister's. It was supposed to be just a casual hangout, but things took a turn. Everyone was older than me, and I wanted to fit in, to show I wasn't some little kid who needed looking after. They kept passing around a joint, nudging me to try it. At first, I held my ground, saying no, thinking about all those anti-drug talks I had heard at school.

But as the night dragged on and the peer pressure kept building, I finally gave in. It was around 4 am in the morning when I took my first puff. That high hit me like a ton of bricks, a strange mix of euphoria and dizziness. I laughed so hard I could barely breathe, eventually passing out on the couch, giggling myself to sleep.

That was the beginning of my complicated relationship with drugs and alcohol. I didn't realize it at the time, but something in me had changed forever. I had crossed a line I couldn't uncross, and I was never quite the same after that.

The days that followed were a blur. I started seeking out that feeling again, that escape from reality. I was still just a kid, but I felt like I had unlocked some kind of secret door to a world where nothing could hurt me.

My friends and I would pool our money to buy cheap liquor and weed, sneaking around behind our parents' backs, thinking we were invincible. It was exhilarating, dangerous, and it quickly became a habit that I couldn't shake.

## Influenced by the Big Screen

Around that same time, I remember watching the movie *The Mack* at the local theater. That film was a game-changer for me. The flashy cars, the money, the power, the way those guys walked and talked—it was like nothing I had ever seen before. They were living a life far removed from my reality in Atlanta, but it was a life I suddenly wanted for myself. As I walked out of that theater, I felt a surge of confidence, like I was already on my way to becoming someone important. I made a promise to myself right then and there: "I'm gonna make it big somehow." I didn't know how, but I knew I was going to find a way.

That movie lit a fire in me, giving me this strange, misplaced sense of ambition. I started paying more attention to the guys in my neighborhood who had nice cars and flashy clothes. They weren't working nine-to-five jobs; they were hustling, making their own rules, and living on their own terms. I watched and learned, trying to figure out what it would take for me to get that kind of respect.

## Life Through Sports and Struggles

Despite my growing interest in the streets, sports remained a huge part of my life. It was one of the few things that kept me grounded. I was good at it, and I loved the attention that came with being the star player. On the football field, I was the quarterback; on the basketball court, a shooting guard; and on the baseball diamond, a first baseman. By the 8th grade, I was a standout athlete, the kind of kid coaches loved to brag about. Everyone at school knew me as the "pretty boy" athlete, and I leaned into it. If everyone else wore black shoes, I wore white. If the other guys had afros, I'd straighten my hair, just to stand out. My uncle used to tease me, saying, "He can play, but he's gotta look cute doing it." It was all part of my persona—different, confident, untouchable.

But as much as I loved sports, high school brought its own set of challenges. By the 11th grade, my focus started slipping. The temptations I had dabbled in as a young teenager were becoming a bigger part of my life. I was hanging with the wrong crowd, spending more time chasing girls, getting high, and partying than I was practicing my jump shot or working on my footwork.

The turning point came during a pick-up football game on a rough patch of pavement. I was showing off, trying to impress some girls who were watching, when I got tackled hard. I hit the ground, skidding across the rough surface, leaving me with scrapes and bruises that went deeper than just the skin. That was the first time I realized I wasn't invincible. The pain lingered, affecting my performance on the field and the court. My coach noticed the difference right away. "Daugherty was good; don't know what happened to him," I overheard him telling another coach one day. That hurt more than the scrapes on my knees. I was losing my edge, and everyone could see it.

## The Downward Spiral

Instead of doubling down on my training, I turned to the streets for the sense of belonging and confidence I was starting to lose in sports. I found myself skipping practice to hang out with my new friends, the ones who were more interested in making quick money and living fast than in chasing a high school diploma. We would drive around the city, looking for trouble, drinking and smoking, acting like we owned the world.

By the time I was 16, I was juggling two lives. At school, I was still trying to keep up the image of the star athlete, the good kid with a promising future. But after hours, I was running wild, chasing thrills and getting deeper into things I knew I shouldn't be messing with. I was still playing football, but my heart wasn't in it anymore. I'd show up hungover or exhausted from a night of partying, my performance suffering more and more. It wasn't long before my coaches stopped expecting much from me, and I stopped expecting much from myself.

One night, after a big game where I had completely messed up, missing crucial plays and letting my team down, I found myself alone in the locker room, staring at my reflection in a cracked mirror. I didn't recognize the person looking back at me. That boy who had dreamed of making it big in sports, of escaping the struggles of his home life, was gone. In his place was someone lost, caught between the world of the athlete and the lure of the streets.

Despite everything, I couldn't bring myself to fully let go of sports. It was the one thing that still tied me to a sense of purpose, however fragile. But the streets had a stronger pull, promising a quicker path to the life I thought I wanted. The money, the power, the respect—it was all within reach if I was willing to take the risks.

As high school neared its end, I found myself at a crossroads, torn between the athlete I used to be and the hustler I was becoming. The streets were calling, and I was ready to answer, no matter the cost.

# Chapter 3

# The Road to Redemption

## The First Taste of Parenthood

In 1978, I became a father for the first time. The moment I held my daughter, a wave of conflicting emotions hit me. On the one hand, I was excited about the idea of having a child, but on the other, I was scared of the responsibilities I knew I wasn't ready for. Her grandmother despised me, and I couldn't blame her. I was a young man whose life was heading nowhere good, caught between wild aspirations and reckless actions.

To complicate matters, another young lady was also pregnant with my child around the same time. I felt embarrassed but oddly proud, as if having multiple kids from different women somehow made me a "big man." I didn't realize the shame it brought to them—or to myself.

While juggling two children from different women, I met another girl and decided to escape the chaos by moving to South Florida. Her family had money—real money. They owned property, ran a taxi company, even a club. They set us up nicely: a house, a job for her, and a chance at stability. But I squandered that opportunity. Instead of building a life, I fell deeper into the party scene. Drugs, liquor, and late nights became my new normal. I was living the high life but couldn't see I was spiraling into a deeper mess.

One day, fueled by a mix of guilt and impulsiveness, I proposed to her. She said yes, and for a fleeting moment, I thought I could change. But deep down, I knew I wasn't ready for marriage or the life that came with it.

I flew back to Atlanta, hoping to figure things out. My mother forced me to break the news to her directly, so I called. Her mother answered, and I blurted out, "I'm sorry, but I can't marry her." The hurt and confusion in her voice was like a dagger to my conscience, but it was too late to turn back.

Years later, I tried to make amends, even helped her through her own struggles, but the damage was done. I had left another broken heart in my wake.

## The Drug Game Beckons

By 19, my life took another dark turn. I was dating an older woman, a 27-year-old who introduced me to a world of luxury, wild parties, and unending drugs. I thought I was on top of the world, but really, I was digging my own grave. That's when my cousin Tony came into the picture. He pulled up in a shiny Cadillac, offering me a way into the lucrative world of drug dealing. He said, "You want real money? This is how you get it." I was hooked on the idea of quick cash and no longer living paycheck to paycheck.

Tony mentored me, showing me the ropes of the cocaine business. I became his runner, transporting kilos from Miami to Atlanta, hiding the stash in secret compartments of rental cars. The money was flowing in, but it came with a cost—I was constantly looking over my shoulder, fearing the police or rival dealers. I couldn't even spend the money openly because that kind of flash would draw too much attention. Still, the allure of the lifestyle kept me locked in. I loved the thrill of it all.

During those wild years, I fathered two more children with different women. One was a sweet girl from Memphis who had dreams of a better life. I could have supported her, could have been there for our child, but instead, I left her behind. I convinced myself that staying away was for their benefit, but deep down, I knew I was only running from responsibility.

## The Glamorous Trap

As I went deeper into the game, I found myself rubbing elbows with major players—dealers, pimps, and hustlers who had no boundaries. I was living a life most people could only dream of: riding in luxury cars, staying in five-star hotels, wearing designer clothes straight from New York. I was living large, but the price of that lifestyle was my soul. My aunt in New York, a woman who had seen it all, would pull me aside and warn, "They'll find you dead out here if you're not careful." But I was too far gone to listen. I was addicted to the rush, meeting dangerous people, making shady deals, always trying to stay one step ahead of disaster.

One night, I got mixed up with a big-time pimp who offered me one of his girls. I took her in, and we started living together, drifting from one hotel to another until we finally got our own place. It seemed like everything was coming together, but danger was always lurking. I'll never forget the night another pimp showed up at our door, waving a gun. He was ready to kill us both, but somehow, I managed to talk him down. We sat there, sharing stories over lines of coke, the gun resting on the table between us. He confessed that he had planned to kill us but changed his mind after talking with me. It was a close call, one of many that should have been a wake-up call.

## Losing and Finding Family

Amidst all the chaos, that girl and I had a child. But I knew I couldn't raise her in that life. I drove my baby daughter to my father and stepmother's house, asking them to take her in. My stepmother agreed but warned me, "Don't you dare come back to take her." She was right; I couldn't keep dragging my daughter through my mess. It broke my heart, but I wanted to give her a chance at a better life, even if it meant giving her up.

Years later, after a stint in prison, I went to see my daughter. She was around eight years old by then. I tried to explain who I was and why I had made the choices I did. But she looked at me with eyes far older than her years and said, "I don't want to hurt anyone by leaving." That crushed me. I had hoped she would want to live with me, to give us a second chance, but I knew deep down that she was right where she needed to be. I had made my choices, and now I had to live with the consequences.

## Realizing the Cost of My Choices

The years I spent chasing money, women, and status left a trail of broken relationships and shattered dreams. I had hurt so many people, some who genuinely cared about me. As I looked back, I realized I had been running from one thing to another, never stopping to face the damage I was causing. It took losing everything—my freedom, my family, my self-respect—for me to finally understand the gravity of my actions.

The turning point came when I found myself alone, sitting in a prison cell, stripped of all the luxuries I once thought defined me. I had no more fancy cars, no women to distract me, no drugs to numb the pain. All I had was time to think and reflect on the choices I made. I realized then that I was the only one to blame for the mess I was in. I had been given chances to change, to do better, but I had squandered them all.

And so, in that cold cell, I made a promise to myself and to God. If I ever got another chance, I would do right. I would find a way to redeem myself, not just for me but for all the people I had hurt along the way. I would find a way to become the man I was meant to be, not the one I had allowed myself to become. It was the beginning of a long journey to redemption, one that I'm still walking to this day.

# Chapter 4

# A Vision in the Darkness

## The Beginning of the End

I had just welcomed my fifth child into the world when everything I had been running from finally caught up with me. The life I was living— filled with fast money, drugs, and fleeting thrills— was a ticking time bomb. One day, as I was lounging in my apartment, a call came in. It was from a guy looking for two kilograms and four ounces of cocaine. My friend T was there, trying to talk some sense into me. "Ron, we don't need to make that run—we got enough money," he pleaded. But I had a different plan. I could already picture myself behind the wheel of a brand-new BMW 525 and my girl, a schoolteacher, living in the house I would buy. This deal, I thought, would set us up for life. Ignoring T's warnings, I set off for Birmingham, Alabama, ready to meet the buyer and secure my dreams.

The plan unraveled the moment I arrived. The buyer wasn't there, so I called him. "Pull up behind the store," he instructed. I followed his directions, thinking I was just moments away from closing the deal. But as soon as I parked, it was like a scene from a movie—police cars swarmed out of nowhere, blocking me in from every direction. For a split second, I thought it was a setup for a robbery. I heard shouts: "Get out of the car!" and "Where's the gun?" I tried to stay calm and yelled back, "I don't have no gun!" But there was no talking my way out of this. One officer shouted, "I got the drugs!" That was it. They slapped the cuffs on me and hauled me off to jail. I was now looking at a potential 15 years of state time and 45 years federal.

## The High Cost of Freedom

After about a month behind bars, I managed to get out on a $100,000 bond, thanks to my attorney. Until that point, I had only ever spent a night in jail—never days, weeks, or months. This was my first serious brush with the law, my first felony conviction. My attorney kept asking if the cops had hurt me during the arrest, as if it were some kind of rite of passage. "You're lucky," he said when I told him they hadn't roughed me up. "They should have."

You would think facing serious prison time would have scared me straight, but instead, I went right back to the lifestyle. Drugs, parties, and women consumed me. One night, I visited a lady who sold liquor out of her house. She looked at me, seeing right through the front I was putting up, and said, "You don't have to do a single day in prison." I didn't understand what she meant, but I wasn't about to stick around to find out. In my mind, maybe she knew some voodoo or something that could help me beat the case. I grabbed a couple of shots, paid her, and left quickly.

## Desperate for Redemption

A few days later, someone introduced me to a church lady who supposedly had a gift. They said she could see things, predict things. Out of options and desperate, I decided to visit her. She shuffled her cards and laid them out, but I never looked too closely at what she was doing. I just needed some sort of answer, some glimmer of hope. She asked why I was there, and I told her, "I need to get off drugs." She gave me a homemade remedy and pointed me to a chapter in the Bible to read. Each time I visited, she told me that my card kept falling on a seven. "You're going to do some prison time," she warned, "but it won't be long—you'll come out okay."

I clung to her words as my trial date approached. When the day finally came, the judge surprised me. "You seem like a good kid," he said, studying me as if he saw something in me worth saving. Then he leaned in and asked if I knew his brother-in-law. I don't remember how I responded, but his tone shifted. "Don't you ever send anyone to my house asking for favors for you," he said sternly. "Do you understand?" I nodded, my heart sinking. My attorney then asked if I could have a few days to get my affairs in order before starting my sentence. The judge granted me five days.

## A Last Attempt at Freedom

I returned to my girlfriend's place, where I spiraled into one last binge. For three days straight, I smoked cocaine, barely eating or sleeping. On the third day, my girlfriend confronted me. "You've been sitting here for three days, not doing anything to help yourself," she said, frustration clear in her eyes. Her words cut through the haze, and I broke down. I cried like a child, the reality of my situation crashing over me. Mama, how could I be so stupid? I thought. That was my rock bottom, and in that moment of despair, I decided I was done with drugs.

The following Sunday, I found myself in church, sitting in the back pew, tears streaming down my face as the choir sang. I felt something stir within me—a small flicker of hope, a whisper that maybe, just maybe, I could turn things around. I listened to the preacher, hanging on every word, knowing that come Monday, I had to face my reality and turn myself in.

**The Fork in the Road**

That night, two big-time players in the drug game came to see me. They laid out a plan that would let me disappear, change my identity, and live somewhere far away. "You'll never see your mama again," they said. For a moment, I considered it. The idea of running away, of escaping the mess I had created, was tempting. But I couldn't do it. I couldn't leave my family behind like that.

On a cold Monday morning in March of 1988, I turned myself into Jefferson County Jail. After a few days, they transferred me to Alabama's diagnostic center in Wetumpka. I went through the usual routine: strip down, wash off, and get handed a prison uniform. They gave me a number—149461. From that moment on, my name was just a series of digits.

## A New Kind of Survival

They assigned me a bed across from an old man who had been locked up for 50 years. He had seen it all, and when I asked him for advice, he said only one thing: "Hear and don't hear, see and don't see." I didn't understand it at the time, but I would soon learn that in prison, that's how you survive.

Draper Correctional Facility became my new home. In a place filled with violence and despair, I sought refuge in the chapel. I went to church every day, praying to God to keep my mind intact. There were nights when I felt like my brain was being wrung out like a wet towel. I'd lie there, pulling the thin prison blanket over my head, whispering, "God, please let me keep my mind. If you do, I'll serve you till I die." For the next 30 days, I didn't miss a single service. An inmate pastor once told me, "You're already saved; you just don't know it yet." I kept coming back, searching for something—maybe redemption, maybe peace. I even joined the choir, losing myself in the music, hoping it would drown out the regrets that haunted me.

Those first months in prison were some of the hardest I'd ever faced. Every day was a struggle to hold on to the pieces of myself that hadn't been completely lost to the streets, the drugs, and the life I had chosen. But for the first time in a long while, I felt like maybe I had a chance to change.

# Chapter 5

# From Chains to Purpose

## A Vision in the Darkness

While waiting for my federal trial in Jefferson County Jail, I found myself trapped not just by the bars around me but by the weight of my past decisions. I was battling more than just the fear of a long sentence; I was battling my own demons. One night, after wrestling with a pounding headache that wouldn't go away, I drifted off into a restless sleep. That's when I had the dream—one that would forever change the course of my life.

In the dream, I was surrounded by people chanting ominously, "He's not gonna make it." Their voices echoed in my mind, and I felt a heaviness in my chest, as if I were suffocating. Suddenly, my body began to float, and I found myself on a wooden dock, alone and exposed. The wind howled, whipping around me, growing stronger by the second. Out of nowhere, two horses came charging toward me, their hooves pounding the ground like a drumbeat. Just as quickly as they appeared, one horse vanished, and the other stumbled, its legs falling off and landing beside me in the dirt.

I felt a surge of desperation and dropped to my knees, praying for the wind to stop. And miraculously, it did. The air grew still, almost eerily so, and I pleaded with God to restore the broken horse. I watched in awe as its legs reattached themselves, piece by piece. The horse swayed, uncertain at first, then gained strength, rocking back and forth before bolting away at full speed. The ground shook as it galloped off, and I was left standing there, stunned. In that moment, a powerful sense of peace washed over me, and I heard a voice in my spirit saying, This is your ministry. You will face many storms, but I will give you the power to calm them. Like that horse, you will be broken but made whole again. One day, you will run free.

When I woke up, I was no longer the same man. The dream lingered in my mind, stirring something deep within me. It felt like a calling, a glimpse of the purpose I had been searching for all my life. For the first time in years, I felt hope, a belief that maybe, just maybe, there was a way out of the darkness I had created.

**Finding My Calling Behind Bars**

Back at Draper Correctional Facility, life was still grim, but I had a new resolve. I found solace in the small group of believers who gathered in the prison chapel. It wasn't much—just a handful of men trying to find redemption in a place built to break us—but it was enough. I started volunteering as a doorkeeper for the makeshift church, greeting everyone who came through. It seemed like a small role, but it gave me purpose.

One afternoon, after a long day of labor, I sat on my bunk and drifted into another dream. This time, I saw myself standing in front of a congregation, preaching the 23rd Psalm. The words flowed from my mouth as if I had known them all my life. When I woke, I couldn't shake the feeling that it was more than just a dream. And sure enough, the next time I went to the chapel, the inmate pastor called me out, saying, "There's someone here who we all want to hear preach today." I was stunned when everyone pointed at me. With my heart pounding, I walked up to the podium and preached the same sermon I had delivered in my dream. It was like something had taken over me, and for the first time, I felt a sense of peace, like I was finally where I was meant to be.

## A Rocky Return to the Real World

After serving my time, I was released in 1991. Walking out of those prison gates was like stepping into a new world. Freedom was intoxicating, but it was also terrifying. I returned to Montgomery, Alabama, with almost nothing to my name—just two worn suit coats, one pair of pants, and no money in my pocket. I had no job, no prospects, and no plan. But I had faith, and that was something I had never truly known before.

I took whatever work I could find, mainly construction jobs that paid just enough to keep food on the table. My wife at the time was losing patience; she wanted stability, not struggle. But I knew I couldn't go back to the life that had landed me in prison. I was determined to stay on the path that God had shown me, no matter how hard it was.

## Breaking Old Chains

One day, I decided to fast for 24 hours—no food, no water, nothing but prayer. It was one of the hardest things I had ever done. But when the fast ended, I realized something incredible: I hadn't smoked in 24 hours. That was a miracle in itself because cigarettes had been my constant companion for years. Then I heard a voice, as clear as if someone were standing next to me, saying, If you can go one day without smoking, you can go the rest of your life. From that moment on, I never picked up another cigarette. April 1, 1988, became the day I left that old habit behind for good.

## Building a New Life and Ministry

By 1996, life had taken me to Atlanta, Georgia, where I felt a new chapter of my life beginning. I started a small Bible study and outreach program, gathering people from the streets and feeding the hungry. It wasn't much, but it was a start. We held our meetings in a cramped 22x14 room with no heat and no air conditioning. We paid $25 a month for that little space, but to me, it felt like a palace. It was the foundation of something bigger, something meaningful.

As the months passed, our little group grew. We eventually managed to purchase the entire building for $80,000. It took every bit of faith and determination I had, but we renovated that place with our own hands, turning it into a true house of worship. The church became a sanctuary for those who had been lost, just like I once was. It grew from a small gathering into a thriving community, a testament to the power of faith and perseverance.

## Running Toward a New Purpose

Looking back, I see how every trial, every mistake, and every dark moment led me to where I am now. The dream I had in that cold jail cell wasn't just a figment of my imagination; it was a promise of what was to come. I had been broken, but like the horse in my vision, I was made whole again. I was given a second chance to run, not away from my past, but toward a future filled with purpose.

Every day, I am reminded that storms will come, but I am no longer afraid. I have faced the consequences of my actions, but I have also found redemption. And with each step I take, I move closer to the man I was always meant to be—a man of faith, a leader, a servant. My journey has been far from easy, but it has been worth every struggle, every tear, and every prayer. This is just the beginning of the life I was truly meant to live.

# Chapter 6

# The Motherland's Call

## Preaching to the Children of the Motherland

When I first embarked on the journey of taking my ministry international, I had no idea just how far God would take me. It was more than I could have ever dreamed, from the islands of the Caribbean to the vast, untamed landscapes of Africa. The first time I set foot on Kenyan soil, it was like stepping into a vivid dream that I never wanted to end. This was a land I had only seen in pictures, a place I had longed to visit ever since I felt that deep calling in my spirit to spread the Word beyond the familiar borders of my home country.

We traveled far from the city, deep into the bush, to host tent meetings that drew crowds from the surrounding villages. I remember the smell of the earth—rich, red clay that seemed to hold the history of all those who had walked upon it before me. The sun was setting, casting a golden glow over the horizon as we pulled up to the large, white tent that had been set up for the revival. The air was thick with anticipation; you could feel the electricity in the air, a palpable sense of excitement that something miraculous was about to happen.

I have a phrase that has become synonymous with my ministry: I got it. It's a declaration of faith, a proclamation that even before the blessing manifests, you claim it with all your heart. That phrase has carried me through my toughest times, and it's something I teach to every congregation I minister to. As we approached the tent that evening, the driver suddenly pointed out the window and told us to look. I turned my head and saw something that nearly brought me to my knees. Across the field, a line of children—barefoot, with beaming smiles—were running toward us, chanting, "I got it! I got it!" with all the joy their little hearts could muster.

Tears filled my eyes as I watched these young souls, so full of life and spirit, repeating the very words that had given me strength. It was as if God Himself was showing me the power of His promise, a living testament to the reach of His Word. These children, on the other side of the world, had embraced a message I had spoken thousands of miles away, and it had ignited a fire in their hearts. In that moment, I realized that my ministry was no longer confined to the four walls of a church; it was spreading like wildfire, touching lives in ways I had never imagined. To see those precious children of the motherland echoing my words was a gift, a confirmation that I was walking in my divine purpose.

## Venturing Alone into the Heart of the Congo

After a successful mission in Kenya, it was time to move on to the next leg of my journey. This time, I was headed to the Democratic Republic of the Congo. My Kenyan travel companions, who had become like family to me, stayed behind, and I found myself traveling alone for the first time. As the plane touched down in Kinshasa, I felt a mix of excitement and apprehension. I had heard stories of the Congo's beauty and its challenges, and I was stepping into it with nothing but my faith to guide me. A wise pastor in Nairobi had reassured me before I left, saying, "You'll be fine in Congo. God's got you." I held onto those words as I navigated this new chapter of my journey.

When I arrived, I was greeted with a reception that I could only describe as royal. Cameras flashed, journalists and media crews surrounded me, and church leaders came out to welcome me as if I were an old friend. It was overwhelming but in the most humbling way. I had always known that God would use me, but I never expected this kind of reception. My host was quick to put me at ease, assuring me that despite the language barrier—this being a French-speaking nation—they would take good care of me.

During my first press interview, a female journalist asked me questions that probed deep into my journey of faith. She was kind, respectful, and curious. Afterward, they whisked me away to my first church service in the Congo. As I stepped out of the car, I was met with a gesture I will never forget— men were laying their suit jackets on the ground for me to walk on. This was a Congolese custom to honor guests, and it left me speechless. I had never experienced anything like it; their hospitality was unlike anything I had ever known. It reminded me that despite our differences in culture and language, the love of Christ can bridge any gap.

## Discovering Riches Beyond Imagination

One of the most unexpected surprises of my journey through the Congo was the stark contrast between poverty and wealth. People often talk about the Congo as one of the poorest countries in the world, but what I saw was a land of immense richness—not just in natural resources but in spirit and resilience. As I was escorted from one church to another, I witnessed grand church buildings with intricate designs that could rival those of any cathedral I'd seen in the West. These churches were not just places of worship; they were community hubs, bustling with life and activity.

One evening, I was invited to dine with one of the president's advisors. As we sat down for dinner, our conversation flowed from the mundane to the extraordinary. We talked about fishing, boats, and eventually, the subject of diamonds came up. I had heard of the Congo's famous diamond mines, but nothing could prepare me for what happened next. The advisor reached into his pocket, pulled out a small cloth, and carefully unwrapped it to reveal a handful of black diamonds. I had never seen anything like them. They sparkled in the dim light, a symbol of the hidden wealth beneath the Congo's troubled surface. It was a moment that made me realize just how much potential lay within this nation, not just in its resources but in its people.

## A Ministry of Hope Amidst Poverty

Yes, there was poverty—unimaginable poverty. I saw it in the eyes of children begging on the streets, in the makeshift homes constructed from scrap metal and plastic. But I also saw hope. I saw it in the faces of the congregants who filled the church pews, eager to hear the Word of God. I saw it in the pastors who led their flocks with unwavering faith despite their own hardships.

I realized that my mission was not just to preach; it was to bring hope, to show them that even in the midst of struggle, they could declare, "I got it," and believe it with every fiber of their being.

My time in the Congo was a testament to the power of faith, resilience, and the indomitable human spirit. I went there expecting to minister to others, but in truth, they ministered to me. They showed me a side of God's grace that I had never known—a grace that thrives even in the harshest conditions, a love that shines brightest in the darkest corners.

As I boarded the plane to leave the Congo, I carried with me not just memories but lessons that would shape the rest of my ministry. Africa had given me a gift that I could never repay—the gift of seeing God's hand at work in the most unexpected places.

The journey had not just been about spreading the gospel; it was about witnessing the gospel in action, seeing lives transformed, and being transformed myself in the process.

Africa had called, and I had answered. And in doing so, I found a piece of my own soul that I never knew was missing.

# Chapter 7

# The Struggles of Ministry

## Running from the Call

If I'm completely honest, my life has been a long journey of running from the calling God placed on me. It's strange to think about it now, especially given the path my life eventually took, but for many years, I was determined to stay as far from ministry as I could. Back when I lived in Smyrna, Georgia, I attended Mount Paran Church of God—a large, bustling church where I could blend into the background. I loved the anonymity it afforded me. I was content to be just another face in the crowd, attending service, worshipping quietly, and going about my business. My focus was on building a career and making money. Ministry was the last thing on my mind.

But God had other plans. One Sunday, after service, the children's church pastor approached my then-wife and me. He said with a big smile, "You two look like a happy couple. Would you like to teach children's church?" Before I could say a word, my wife blurted out, "He's a minister." I was taken aback. Inside, I was screaming, "Why'd she say that?" I had worked so hard to keep that part of my life tucked away. But God, in His relentless pursuit, had a way of putting me exactly where He wanted me, even when I was running full speed in the opposite direction.

A few weeks later, there I was, standing in front of a group of children, teaching Bible lessons and wondering how I had gotten myself into this situation. Every Sunday, I would wrestle with the feeling of being out of place, yet somehow, I couldn't deny the peace that came with doing what I knew, deep down, I was called to do. It wasn't long before I found myself fully immersed in children's ministry, and as much as I resisted, I could feel God's hand guiding me, pulling me deeper into His purpose.

Dr. Paul Walker, the senior pastor of Mount Paran, had a profound impact on me during those years. His sermons were powerful, each message feeling like it was crafted just for me. I remember sitting in the pews, trying to be invisible, only for his words to pierce straight through my heart. It was as if God was using Dr. Walker to speak directly to me, challenging me to step into the role He had prepared for me. Years later, when Dr. Walker came to preach at my own ministry's anniversary service, it was a full-circle moment. I stood there in awe, humbled by the journey God had taken me on, from the reluctant attendee to a pastor with a ministry of my own.

## A Leap of Faith

The path to building a church was far from easy. For twelve long years, we operated out of a tiny storefront space. I poured everything I had into that ministry, but it seemed like no matter how hard we tried, we just couldn't break free from those four walls. There were days when I questioned whether I was truly walking in God's will, but I held onto the vision He had given me.

It wasn't until one day, out of the blue, that my bishop called me. His voice was serious as he said, "The Holy Spirit has convicted me. I should have given you my old church building, but I didn't.

Don't be afraid to take the property that's coming up. Don't worry about the cost. God will provide."

That conversation set off a chain of events I could have never predicted. Within months, we were faced with the opportunity to purchase a $1.2 million property. It felt impossible. We were a small congregation with limited resources, but I remembered my bishop's words: "Don't worry about the cost." It was a test of faith, a moment where I had to trust that God would make a way where there seemed to be no way. We took the leap, signed the papers, and began the journey of transforming that property into a place of worship. It was a lesson that ministry is not just built on hard work but on unwavering faith—believing in things you can't yet see, trusting that God's promises are true.

We faced challenges at every turn—financial hurdles, construction delays, and moments of doubt that threatened to derail the whole project. But each time, God showed up in ways that left us in awe. One day, during a particularly difficult period, I received a call from a donor who had heard about our work and wanted to contribute a substantial amount. That donation covered the exact amount we needed to complete the next phase of renovations. It was as if God was reminding me that He is the ultimate provider, the One who opens doors no man can shut.

## Miracles in the Making

The early days of our ministry were marked by a series of small miracles that confirmed we were on the right path. I remember we had no musicians, no choir, just a deep desire to worship. We prayed fervently, declaring that God would send the right people. We even went so far as to buy instruments before we had anyone to play them. It was an act of faith, speaking into the atmosphere that God would bring musicians our way. And sure enough, not long after, a group of young, talented musicians showed up at our door, ready to serve. We called them "One Sound," and they became an integral part of our church's worship experience.

But it wasn't just about building the physical church. We were also believing God for land. I had a vision of a sprawling campus where we could expand our ministry beyond Sunday services. We prayed for 15 acres and ended up securing 13.7—close enough to the vision God had given us. It was a reminder that while we may not always get exactly what we ask for, God's provision is always more than enough.

Then came the test of my personal faith. In 2020, I contracted COVID-19. The virus hit me hard, and I struggled to breathe. My family was worried, urging me to go to the hospital, but I refused. I turned to God in my weakest moment and said, "Lord, if You don't heal me, I'm ready to go home. But if it's Your will, I know You can make me whole."

I isolated myself in prayer and fasting, believing with every ounce of my being that God would come through. And He did. Within days, my symptoms began to ease, and I made a full recovery. It was a personal testimony of God's healing power—a testament to the fact that faith isn't just something you preach; it's something you live.

## Enduring the Struggles

Despite the victories, there were also many struggles. The weight of leading a ministry can be overwhelming. There were times when I questioned whether I was truly cut out for this, moments when the burden felt too heavy to bear. But each challenge brought me closer to God, reminding me that in my weakness, His strength is made perfect. Ministry isn't glamorous; it's filled with long nights, financial strain, and the emotional toll of caring for people who look to you for guidance.

But it's also filled with the joy of seeing lives transformed, the thrill of watching God move in miraculous ways, and the deep satisfaction of knowing you are walking in your divine purpose. Each struggle, each setback, was a stepping stone to something greater, a preparation for the next chapter in the journey.

Looking back, I see now that running from the call was never an option. God's hand was upon me, guiding me, even when I didn't realize it. The struggles of ministry have shaped me, refined me, and brought me to a place of deeper faith. It's a journey I wouldn't trade for anything in the world because through it all, I've seen the hand of God move in ways I could have never imagined.

# Chapter 8

# Navigating New Beginnings

## Hitting Rock Bottom

In 2018, my world came crashing down. After 29 years of marriage, my wife and I divorced, a reality I never thought I would face. I had built a life centered around my family, ministry, and the church. I had given everything I had to my congregation, my marriage, and my community, only to find myself broken, exhausted, and utterly lost. The end of my marriage left me grappling with questions that had no easy answers. The pain of separation was a wound that cut deeper than I could have ever imagined.

The final conversation with my ex-wife still plays vividly in my mind. It was after a Sunday service, and I could see the tension in her eyes. She confronted me with accusations—claims that I had let another woman from the church get too close. I tried to explain that it was all a misunderstanding, but she was convinced otherwise. She told me to leave, and in that moment, I felt my entire world collapse. I was blindsided, left in a state of shock, unable to comprehend how things had spiraled so out of control.

For months, I was a wanderer, staying wherever I could find a place to rest my head. At first, I stayed in the church's family life center, sleeping on a small cot in the back room. The same church where I had spent years pouring out my heart was now my temporary refuge. After a while, I moved in with my youngest daughter, grateful for her kindness but still feeling like a burden. Eventually, I knew I had to reclaim my independence. I rented a small apartment, purchased new furniture, and slowly began to rebuild my life from the ground up.

For the first time in decades, I was living alone. The silence of those empty rooms was both a comfort and a curse. It was a chance to reflect, to heal, but it also meant facing the reality of my situation. To cope, I threw myself into new experiences—dating, traveling, even buying a sleek, red convertible that I had always dreamed of but never allowed myself to enjoy. It was the first taste of freedom I'd had in years, yet it was bittersweet. I was free, but at what cost? I was learning to live for myself, but the loneliness was always lurking just beneath the surface.

Then came the pandemic in 2020, turning the world upside down. The freedoms I had just begun to explore were suddenly stripped away. Funerals became the mainstay of my ministry work as COVID-19 took lives by the hundreds. Week after week, I stood over caskets, delivering eulogies for those who had succumbed to the virus. It felt like a never-ending cycle of grief. I began to ask my mother if I was next. The weight of loss, both personal and communal, was overwhelming. It was a dark time, one where I often found myself questioning not just my purpose, but my very existence.

## An Unexpected Encounter

In the midst of this bleak season, I had an encounter that would forever change my perspective. One night during the height of the pandemic, I pulled into the Toco Hills shopping center, intending to grab some takeout. As I parked my convertible, a disheveled homeless man approached me. "Don't park there, sir. You'll get towed," he warned. I was taken aback by his concern for me, a complete stranger. Curious, I went inside to verify his warning, and sure enough, he was right.

When I came back out, I saw him waiting for me. I thanked him for the heads-up, and he offered to guide me to a safer parking spot. As we walked, he began to share bits and pieces of his life story. He spoke of his younger days, how he and his brother would sing gospel songs in churches, their grandmother proudly taking them from one congregation to another. There was a wistfulness in his voice, a longing for a past that was long gone. To my surprise, he suddenly broke into song, right there in the parking lot. His voice was soulful, filled with emotion, resonating with a beauty that belied his worn appearance. It was as if for a brief moment, we were transported out of the chaos of the world and into a sacred space.

After his song, he looked at me with eyes that seemed to peer into my soul. "I need $26 to get a tooth pulled," he said, almost as an afterthought. I reached into my pockets, but I had no cash on me. I promised him I would return on Sunday to help him out. Before we parted, he asked if he could pray for me. This man, who had nothing, was offering to pray for me. How could I say no? I bowed my head, and as he prayed, something inside me shifted. He began to prophesy, declaring that God wasn't finished with me yet. His words were like a balm to my wounded spirit, and tears welled up in my eyes. I fought to keep them from falling, not wanting anyone to see my vulnerability.

As I walked away, I heard a whisper in my spirit, a voice urging me to go back and give him the money now, to bless him without delay. I turned around, but he was gone. I searched up and down the lot, but it was as if he had vanished into thin air. I stood there, bewildered, a sense of awe washing over me. I truly believe he was an angel, sent to remind me that even in the midst of my darkest days, God still had a plan for me. That encounter was a turning point, a divine reminder that I was not alone, that my story wasn't over.

## Finding Purpose in Pain

Life after divorce was a journey of rediscovery. The freedom I thought I wanted came with unexpected challenges. I had to learn how to be alone, how to find joy without the constant presence of another person. I took up hobbies I had long neglected, like fishing and painting. I started to explore new places, not just to escape the memories but to create new ones. Yet, no matter how far I traveled or how many new experiences I embraced, there was always a part of me searching for something more.

During this time, I also threw myself into my work. Ministry became my lifeline, the one constant in a world that seemed to be falling apart. But it wasn't just about preaching or leading services; it was about truly connecting with people who were also struggling, who were also trying to find their way through the darkness. I began to see my own pain as a bridge to understanding the pain of others. Every funeral I conducted, every counseling session, every prayer meeting became an opportunity to pour out the comfort that I myself was desperately seeking.

There were still days when the loneliness was overwhelming, when the weight of my past mistakes and regrets threatened to pull me under. But I learned to lean into God's grace, to trust that He was using even my brokenness for His glory. Life after divorce wasn't just about survival; it was about transformation. It was about finding beauty in the ashes, purpose in the pain, and hope in the most unexpected places.

**Embracing New Beginnings**

As I reflect on this chapter of my life, I realize that hitting rock bottom was a blessing in disguise. It stripped away all the things I thought I needed and brought me back to the core of who I am—a child of God, called to serve, even in the midst of my own brokenness. The journey hasn't been easy, but it has been worth it. Each struggle, each encounter, each divine intervention has been a step toward becoming the man God always intended me to be.

Divorce was not the end; it was a new beginning. It was a painful chapter, but one that has taught me resilience, humility, and the power of grace. I am not the same person I was before. I am stronger, wiser, and more determined to live out the calling God has placed on my life. The road ahead is still uncertain, but I face it with a renewed sense of purpose, knowing that no matter what comes my way, I got it.

# Chapter 9

# Holding Onto Faith

## Hitting Financial Rock Bottom

In the early 2000s, I faced one of the most difficult seasons of my life—one that tested not only my faith but my ability to keep moving forward when the odds seemed insurmountable. My ministry's bank accounts had all but dried up, and we were staring down the barrel of insurmountable debt. At that point, I had only $100 left to my name, but our monthly expenses totaled over $24,000. The weight of it all pressed down on me like a vice. How had I let this happen? How had we gotten to this place where the ministry I had poured so much into seemed to be on the brink of collapse?

I remember walking outside one evening, staring up at the sky and complaining to God. I asked Him, "How could You let this happen? How could You let me get this far in over my head?" I was angry, confused, and feeling utterly defeated. It was in that moment of frustration that I heard God speak to my heart, quietly but firmly: "Look around."

I did as He said. I looked at the church building, the family life center, the house, the land — all the things that had come to represent not just the ministry, but my years of hard work, sacrifice, and vision. It was easy to see the financial struggles, the emptiness in the bank account, and the looming threat of failure. But then God spoke again: "Look again. Look in the spirit."

That's when it hit me. I had been so focused on the material world — the bills, the debts, the challenges — that I had forgotten about the lives we had touched, the transformations we had witnessed, and the miracles that had unfolded right before us. Families had been restored. Addicts had been delivered. People had been healed — both physically and spiritually. We had built something that was more than just bricks and mortar; we had built a community, a movement that had made a real impact in the lives of countless people.

In that moment, I understood that God had allowed me to experience the struggle because it was part of His greater plan. If He had shown me all the hardships that would come with ministry, I might have never stepped into it. But through it all, He had been there—guiding, providing, and teaching me lessons that would shape the man I would become.

**Bankruptcy and a Fresh Start**

As the financial strain continued, things came to a head when the bank that had been supportive of our ministry was bought out by a larger institution. We found ourselves in an even more precarious situation, and ultimately, we had no choice but to file for bankruptcy. The word itself felt like a weight I couldn't bear, a label that seemed to define failure. I hesitated, unsure if this was the right move. But God, as always, had a plan.

A real estate attorney I knew encouraged me to go ahead and file. "White folks do this all the time," he said. "Black folks need to understand it's okay." His words resonated with me, but they also challenged me. I had been taught to fear financial setbacks, to see them as personal failures. But God was showing me that bankruptcy wasn't the end—it was a tool for restoration. It was an opportunity to start over, to shed the weight of debt that had been dragging us down for years.

With the help of my attorney, we cleared over $2 million in debts, all while managing to keep our buildings, our furniture, and our equipment. The weight of that financial burden lifted, and for the first time in years, I felt like I could breathe again. The ministry wasn't destroyed. It wasn't the end. It was a fresh start.

But the lessons didn't stop there. After the bankruptcy was finalized, I realized I needed to equip myself with more knowledge. I had always been driven to learn, and this new chapter in my life was no exception. I decided to go back to school. I completed an education degree and even pursued an MBA. It was a season of rebuilding—of retooling my mind, heart, and spirit for the next chapter. It was God's way of showing me that even after years of struggles in ministry and personal heartbreak, life could be rebuilt. God wasn't finished with me yet.

## A New Chapter in Life

These chapters in my story aren't the final ones. I have come to understand that while we go through seasons of hardship, we are never truly finished. God is always at work, molding us, refining us, preparing us for what's next. I had walked through financial ruin, emotional pain, and personal loss, but God's grace had carried me through it all. And just when I thought I had nothing left, He showed me that there was so much more to come.

Looking back, I can see how the struggles I faced weren't random or without purpose. They were the very things that shaped me into who I am today. They taught me to trust God more deeply, to hold onto faith even when everything around me seemed to be crumbling. I learned that God doesn't always work in ways we expect, but His timing is perfect, and His plans are always better than anything we could have imagined.

Through it all, I've learned some key lessons that I hope will resonate with others who find themselves facing similar struggles:

1. Hold onto your faith, even when it feels like everything is falling apart. Life is full of challenges, but faith has a way of seeing us through even the darkest moments. I've learned that God is faithful, even when the situation looks impossible.

2. Embrace failure as a stepping stone, not a setback. The bankruptcy was a painful experience, but it was also a powerful lesson in resilience. Sometimes, our greatest breakthroughs come after our biggest failures.

3. Know that rebuilding is possible. Just because something is broken doesn't mean it can't be restored. I rebuilt not just my financial life, but my personal life as well. Don't give up on yourself or on God's ability to bring restoration.

4. Take time to invest in yourself. Sometimes, the best way to move forward is by equipping yourself with more knowledge and skills. Going back to school wasn't just about getting a degree; it was about preparing for the next phase of life and ministry. Always be open to growth.

5. Trust God's plan, even when you don't understand it. I never could have imagined that bankruptcy would lead me to a fresh start, but it did. God's plan is often far greater than what we can see at the moment. Trust that He knows what He's doing.

Looking ahead, I am excited for the future. God is still working on me, still writing my story, and I am eager to see where He leads me next. These are the last chapters of this particular journey, but I know that the story isn't over. There's still so much to be written. God is faithful, and as long as I keep holding onto Him, I know that my best chapters are yet to come.

## Summary and Key Takeaways:

As I reflect on the key moments of my life, I am struck by the grace, faith, and perseverance that have defined my journey. From the financial ruin that threatened to destroy my ministry to the personal heartbreak of divorce, each challenge was a stepping stone that led me to a place of greater understanding and spiritual depth. I learned to hold onto my faith, even in the hardest moments, and to embrace the possibility of new beginnings after every setback.

Life may not always go according to plan, but with God by your side, you can rebuild and grow stronger from every challenge you face. Hold on to your faith, seek God's guidance in times of crisis, and trust that He will always make a way where there seems to be no way. And when you find yourself in the pit, remember that sometimes, the most beautiful stories come from the darkest places. Keep going—your next chapter might be just around the corner.

# ABOUT THE AUTHOR

Ronald Daugherty represents a testimony to the restorative and transforming nature of God. Through submission to the power of the Holy Spirit, his obedience to follow God's plan for his life, and his willingness to go through the process, God is able to use him mightily. Daugherty is involved in international works and has become a shining light revealing the Lord's divine, redemptive power. Through Christ, he has helped many through restoration and the transformational process.

Daugherty holds a Bachelor of Arts degree in Leadership Studies from Beulah Heights University and an MBA in Communications and Marketing from South University. He also received his Life Coach training from Dream Releasers Coaching.

# CONTACT INFORMATION

**Ronald Daugherty**
**Connecting Point Recovery CDC**

**Phone**
470-558-8855

**Website Address**
https://connecting-point.org

**Email Address**
connect.point@connecting-point.org